Can big things come from small places?

The faithfulness of God!

~Wisdom Series~

S
SIGNATURE PAGE

TO: _____

DATE _____

THANK YOU!

~Wisdom Series~

G

GOLDEN NUGGETS OF WISDOM DEVOTIONAL SERIES

~*COLLECTOR'S EDITION*~

VOLUMES 1-4

~BONUS~
~VITAMINS FOR YOUR VISION~

BRIAN R. DAVIS

Instant Publisher
Collierville, Tennessee

~Wisdom Series~

Published by Brian R. Davis
Duluth, Georgia

Copyright © 2009 Prophet Brian R. Davis

Cover design by Casey McDaniel (Case love Productions)

Book Design by Prophet Brian Davis

Editing by Loretta Blanding-Staff

All rights reserved

No part of this book may be reproduced in any form or by any means without prior written permission of the publisher.

Unless otherwise noted, all scripture quotations are taken from The King James Version of the Holy Bible.

Publisher's Note

All definitions were taken from dictionary.com.
Some scriptures were also taken from e-sword.com.
Copyright 2007 Rick Meyers. All rights reserved.

Printed in the United States of America.

~Wisdom Series~

DEDICATION

To my beautiful wife; **Caressia R. Davis**. You share me with the world as a prophet, a singer, an author, but love me just for being Brian. I love you and hope that the wisdom God has granted me will lead us into many wealthy streams.

To my twins, Deene, Deena and my entire group of God kids, nieces and nephews. May the wisdom in this book be the most valuable inheritance and trusted resource of guidance your life and destiny. I love you!

To **Dr. Mike Murdock**: Oblivious of the fact you had released so many books concerning wisdom and the fact that you have become a major trusted voice and mentor via telecast, I honor you. As I listen to you the anointing on your life causes my spirit to leap within: After which provoking me to pursue by virtue of an insatiable desire to walk in a greater dimension of wisdom and Godly principles. Thank you!

~Wisdom Series~

ACKNOWLEDGEMENTS

To Prophetess Marcia Morrison: You have been an Eli in my life. Your insightful words of wisdom have spoken into areas of my life hat were wounded and dormant. Thank you for covering and helping me to become a more excellent vessel both naturally and spiritually.

Prophetess Juanita Bynum, Bishop Thomas Weeks III, Pastor Lawrence Denning, , Apostle Paul Wondracek, Pastor Odell Jones, Pastors Tyrone and Barbara Powell, Pastors Bobby and Almeta Mack, Pastor Dan and Vallee Jones, Pastors Scott and Tyear McCrary, Pastor Flora White, Pastor Ernie Torri. You have all poured into my life immeasurable proportions of wisdom. Thank you!

Very special thanks to Minister Tim Burges. My life and ministry will never be the same. Your insatiable desire and passion to see a greater level of integrity and honor in the Body of Christ at large has restored my faith. I thank you and Cornerstone Television for being the conduit that God is using to fulfill his word over my life.

~Wisdom Series~

PREFACE

Have you ever made a decision that was not so intelligent? Have you dealt with issues that you had not previously faced and wished that you had made a different choice? Have you ever put yourself in predicaments where soon after you realized that you had made a tremendous error? You say to yourself 'if I knew then what I know now; I would have never done this or that'.

You very seldom fully weigh the long and short term effects of those decisions. In every area of our lives we need wisdom. We can save ourselves much pain, money, frustration and disappointment if it is present and active in our lives. The Bible declares that they who love wisdom shall eat the fruit thereof and ultimately experience increase. May this book enhance your life and provoke you to pursue higher dimensions of wisdom and understanding in God.

Wisdom cries out for us even in the streets and desires to be our safe haven and therapist. Wisdom is to humanity what diamonds are to a coal miner: A hidden treasure that will increase and bring unmeasured prosperity. It is my sincere desire that as you read this book you are provoked to pursue wisdom like never before and allow your understanding to be even more enlightened. May the practical but powerful truths change your life!

CONTENTS

CONTENTS..9

ACCOUNABILITY..12

ANGER...14

DEALING WITH ISSUES 17

DECISIONS..19

DESTINY..25

DETERMINATION...27

DREAMS..31

FAITH...33

FREEDOM..37

GRATITUDE..43

HEALING...45

HUMILITY...47

LEADERSHIP..51

LAZINESS..54

LOVE..56

OBEIDIENCE...58

~Wisdom Series~

PATIENCE..62

PLANS..64

POSSIBILITIES...66

PRAISE...68

PRAYER..71

PRIDE...74

PROCESS...76

PROCRASTINATION...82

PROGRESS...84

PROVISION..87

PURPOSE..89

REJECTION..91

RELATIONSHIPS..93

THINKING..96

TIMING..98

BONUS SERIES-VISION & ENTREPENUER..............101

WISDOM TREASURES...123

NOTES...126

MINISTRY INFO..135

RESOURCE..136

PARTNERSHIP...137

~Wisdom Series~

W

Wisdom is the principal thing;

therefore get wisdom:

and with all thy getting

get understanding.

Proverbs 4:7

~Wisdom Series~

ACCOUNTABILITY

NUGGET 1

To whom much is given, much more is required. To whom little is given, more is also still required.

NUGGET 2

A wise man always protects his present: Because while on the phone with his future his past will keep trying to beep in.
Deny call waiting or be delayed!

NUGGET 3

Sure the ant rests all winter, he worked all summer!
Life is always sweeter when you've earned the right to enjoy the **fruit** of your own labor.

Proverbs 6:6-8
Go to the ant thou sluggard; consider his ways and be wise;

~Wisdom Series~

A
N
G
E
R

~Wisdom Series~

NUGGET 4

Anger is like a red light. When approaching you either stop or wreck lives!

Pray this; Lord help me to have temperance and to allow your peace to be my portion. Help me to consider my ways so that I am not sentenced by them.

NUGGET 5

You don't choose when you will get angry, but you can conclude how you will respond.
Anger is not the sin, your response may be!

NUGGET 6

The size of your tongue is <u>minuscule</u> but its effect can be enormous!

No matter how big the ship, it is controlled by a little wheel.

~ 15 ~

~Wisdom Series~

James 3:5

Likewise the **tongue** *is a small part of the body, but it makes great boasts. Consider what a great forest is set on fire by a small spark.*

NUGGET 6-6

When you are angry serve your words like a slice of hot apple pie; Wait until they cool!

~Wisdom Series~

DEALING WITH ISSUES

NUGGET 7

Public disclosure often comes when private exposure is ignored.

God gives us an opportunity to deal with our issues individually and discretely. When we don't take advantage of this there are often catastrophic consequences.

NUGGET 8

What you don't destroy at the root will return.

What you fail to deal with at the very core of its origin has the potential of being a constant disturbance in your life. It is far better to visit these issues early on or you will most likely receive unexpected visitations in the future.

~Wisdom Series~

DECISIONS

~Wisdom Series~

NUGGET 9

When blessed with opportunities, poverty is a choice, not a social class!
Proverbs 20:4
The sluggard will not plow by reason of the cold; therefore shall he beg in harvest, and have nothing.

NUGGET 10

Apathy makes empty.

As long as you operate without passion, you'll suffer and will have no substance.

NUGGET 11

The person who is never specific, will more than often become a statistic.
2 Timothy 1:7

NUGGET 12

Stupidity is operating the same way, refusing a better way, and expecting a different way.

When you refuse to understand or learn from your experiences, you become responsible for paying tuition for a class you weren't required to take.

NUGGET 13

Beware of the fool who buys his wants, begs his needs and then ask you to pay the difference.

It is one thing to be the answered prayer to someone in need; it is another thing to be the bailout for someone that creates more needs because of greed.

~Wisdom Series~

NUGGET 14

The worst decision is simply not making one!
Every decision costs; but a 50% chance sure looks better than a $0 check.

NUGGET 15

He who leaves right can go back.

The prodigal son's timing may have been off, but his method was right. He had every right to ask for his portion but the honor in which he left made him eligible for a greater portion once he returned!

NUGGET 16

Be careful who you allow to make withdrawals without ever making deposits.

You'll find that you'll soon become insufficient and insignificant.

~Wisdom Series~

NUGGET 17

Things only seem too good to be true when you fail to release what was.

Is what's holding on to you worth forfeiting what wants to come to you? You never can begin to live in what is until you leave the grave sight of what was! RIP.

NUGGET 18

It's never a bad idea to get a second opinion: especially if the first has cost you before.

Proverbs 11:14

Where no wise guidance is, the people fall; but in the multitude of counselors there is safety.

NUGGET 19

A single wrong decision can cost you double.

Proverbs 3:5

Trust in the LORD with all your heart and lean not on your own understanding;

Consultation can prevent unnecessary devastation!

The decision that you make on an impulse, could be the very one to cause you to lose your pulse PERMANATELY!

~Wisdom Series~

_D_

_E_

_S_

_T_

_I_

_N_

_Y_

NUGGET 20

He, who is a great manager of time, is one that will be a great manager of his or her destiny.

NUGGET 21

Surrounding yourself with positive people is like taking vitamins; your resistance to failure becomes stronger.

NUGGET 22

Although Moses complained about his stuttering problem, God did not respond. Why? God is not concerned with your ability or inability, he looks for your availability.

A donkey and a horse have the ability to carry. The problem comes when they won't!

~Wisdom Series~

DETERMINATION

NUGGET 23

Your greatness is not determined by your achievement but by your relentless pursuit despite failures.

NUGGET 24

Einstein, Jordan......... are both names of great and successful individuals who were denied, cast out and rejected! But look what going against all the odds will allow you to accomplish!

> Make every effort to not allow the spirit of rejection to cause you to give up so easily. Persevere through every negative obstacle and turn a deaf ear towards every whisper of disbelief. Walk in faith and do not allow what you see to cause you to fear. Possess the boldness to stand and become the voice of 'YES' in a no society.

~Wisdom Series~

NUGGET 25

Scars produce stars.

Scars are sometimes invisible and sometimes they are not. Yet they speak of personal pain worthy of honor again and again. Show me someone great and I'll show you one that has been through much. Accomplishments are testaments that attract endorsements!

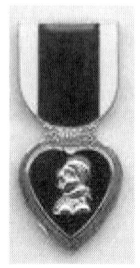 

A SALUTE TO OUR SERVICE MEN & WOMEN

NUGGET 26

Kryptonite is not superman's enemy. It only proves that he's still bigger than his last battle.
When a man is strengthened what use to destroy will become a toy!

NUGGET 27

Don't allow someone else's bad experiences to determine the reality of your good ones.

Be careful when the resentment or pain of another individual about someone or something causes you to be snared. Bitter frustrates and delays better! It is a dangerous thing to allow yourself to be entangled by a web that you didn't spin.

~Wisdom Series~

_D_

_R_

_E_

_A_

_M_

_S_

NUGGET 28

If you always wait for someone else to ignite your dreams, you also give them the power to put them out!

If God gave you the dream then it is a firm indication that he also granted you with the capacity to fulfill it. Never place your dreams in the hands of an individual who does not possess the dexterity or the wherewithal to help you achieve it. Much is to be said about what another person's lack of passion could cost you.

NUGGET 29

Life can and will sometime make plans for you that you had not planned for. Such is life, but how you confront it determines the final outcome.

It is one thing to have a flat; it is another to have a spare.

~Wisdom Series~

_F_

_A_

_I_

_T_

_H_

NUGGET 30

Facts look out, fear looks down, faith looks up.

Sight is required for fact and fear but faith can be blind folded.

NUGGET 31

Faith does not exclude reality;
Faith transcends reality.

Hebrews 11:1

¹Now faith is the assurance of things hoped for, the conviction of things not seen.

F-*FINDING*

A-*ASSURANCE*

I-*INSPITE OF*

T-*THE*

H-*HURDLES*

Faith *is a supernatural answer to a natural challenge. For some, faith has been accredited as nothing less than a bizarre phenomenon. It sees when nothing is there and calls upon that which can't be seen or without surety will respond back. Faith is without doubt the unexplainable witness in your soul that is accompanied by a peace which surpasses all understanding knowing that all is well and is working for your good. Faith is when the elevator of your life is malfunctioning and you immediately look for the stairs. Faith and reason are enemies. Reason asks how, when, what and who but faith says 'JUST DO IT".*

You have to be particular of your surroundings during this time. Your surroundings must consist of people that are true and loyal because someone who does not know you will seize an opportunity to make $100 dollars checking you into the nearest psychiatric facility for insanity. Once you have been an eyewitness to the manifestations of unwavering faith logic has to take a back seat. Believe the impossible and expect the miraculous.

Matthew 17:20

*"I tell you the truth, if you have faith as small as a **mustard seed**, you can say to this mountain, 'Move from here to there' and it will move. Nothing will be impossible for you.*

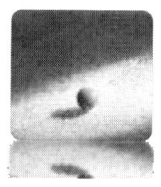

~Wisdom Series~

F

R

E

E

D

O

M

NUGGET 32

Never walk in a door that you can't control its access!

Never allow someone else to trap you in a place that imprisons your freedom. Someone else's door may be your dungeon.

NUGGET 33

If what has held you is still holding on, then what is assigned to you can't belong.

Have you ever looked back at your elementary school photos and saw the picture that captured you being snaggletooth? Many people including you laughed and would rather keep that picture a hidden memory. New tooth can't come up until the old ones come out. What needs to be pulled out so something else can grow in its place? Selah.

~Wisdom Series~

NUGGET 34

Freedom is not only given to you but demanded by you.

Though we live in a country that is free; a country where many travel for miles and miles to start a new life of opportunity and gain a fresh start; there are many things that come to appose such a liberty. In a world where we are blessed with such freedom to my chagrin there are those who still choose to live like a subservient. What is it that is so attractive about bondage? This is such an oxymoron. Why does a battered woman or man stay in this kind of relationship? How much is enough? It's one thing to be held at gun point however it is another to buy the gun! Never allow someone to put you in predicament that strips you of the freedom that rightfully belongs to you. Slavery only submerges the individual that allows it to resurface. Live free!

Why do men and women make detrimental decisions that result in their imprisonment to a confinement institution? As a teacher in the public school system for a year I would always ask myself why a child would prefer 'ISS' or (in school suspension) rather than being apart of a more productive and conducive group of kids?: who took advantage of every moment and readily walked into every open door that would ensure their educational success. While there could be a plethora of answers to these questions there is one sure fact that is crystal clear. Freedom is without a doubt a mind set. It is a decision and an attitude that controls and determines an individual's out come. My propensity to only embrace that which is positive mirrors the story <u>The Little Engine That Could</u>.

~Wisdom Series~

NUGGET 34-Continued

The Little Engine that Could, also known as The Pony Engine, is a moralistic children's story that appeared in the United States of America. The book for many years has been used to teach children the value of optimism and hard work. In the tale, a long train must be pulled over a very high mountain. Much larger engines, treated anthropomorphically, (giving human characteristics to non-human things) are asked to pull the train.

The story chronicles that for various reasons they refused. The request was sent to a small engine, who agrees to try. The engine succeeds in pulling the train over the mountain while repeating its motto: "I-think-I-can". It is clearly evident here that the little engine's positive attitude was the foundation of his ability to do what was thought to e the impossible. With this kind of attitude the tentacles of limitation, bondage and inferiority will in no way possible neither bind nor restrict one's freedom.

Learn to live in the 'free zone'. In the words of the dynamic singers known all over the world as the Clark Sisters; 'The sky is the limit to what you can have'. Allow nothing or no one to handcuff you to anything that will prevent you from walking in a freedom that despite what you have had to endure that causes you to walk in confidence: and with boldness join in with the cloud of witness that were able to say 'Free at last- free at last; Thank God almighty we are free at last'.

~Wisdom Series~

G
R
A
T
I
T
U
D
E

NUGGET 35

Mad about leftovers? Go to the Soup Kitchen. Ungrateful for your house? Try trading places with Bob the Home-less man!

1 Thessalonians 5:18
In every thing give thanks

NUGGET 36

Never be so busy with life that you fail to acknowledge the one who gives it.

My mother taught me that when someone does something for you, the least you can do is to say 'thank you.' My Dad put it like this, 'never forget where you've come from'.

~Wisdom Series~

H

E

A

L

I

N

G

NUGGET 37

An issue concealed, is an issue unhealed.

The woman with the issue of blood would have never been held had she stayed in confinement with everyone else.

NUGGET 38

Why kill just 3 bees and leave the hive? Why mop the floor and not fix the leak?

If you don't deal with a thing in its entirety, then you defeat the purpose of even starting!

NUGGET 39

Laughter is free medicine: it only costs your sadness.
Proverbs 17:22

~Wisdom Series~

_H_
_U_
_M_
_I_
_L_
_I_
_T_
_Y_

NUGGET 40

If you really want to be great, start with a mop!

NUGGET 41

The foundation of true greatness is humility.

1 Peter 5:6

NUGGET 42

When you are assigned to run a race, run will always become ruin when you put 'I' in it.

NUGGET 43

Don't allow your pride to hinder another person's promotion.

NUGGET 43-Continued

I have been rebuked by individuals that wanted to sow into my life, but because of being backstabbed previously I said no. I had to learn that God will send those to help sustain you in hardships, I had to remember that I asked God to help and he sent them as an answer.

NUGGET 44

Servants willingly submit, Serpents intentionally split.

Which one are you?

Division-*Do you promote unity or division? It is one thing to disagree but it is another to divide. My wonderful mother often said to me, 'If you don't agree something then just leave. You do not have to tare the whole thing up because you don't see eye to eye with it'. This is so true. You can agree to disagree as friends but that does not suggest that your friendship is over.*

NUGGET 44-Continued

Submission-You can only be poured into by what or who you are willing submit to. Submitting or yielding to the authority of another is not a curse as many would think! You could be the Queen of England but in order for you to obtain a degree you would have to subject yourself to the instructions and set guidelines required by the professor. Would you be honored by virtue of your social status? Of course but you would still have to abide by the same ordinances. Submission does not degrade nor deduce your power and influence but rather affirms your right to be bestowed with such distinction. You would have a major problem at the dentist, in the operating room or being pulled over by a state patrolman along the interstate; if the essence of submission through humility was not adhered to or properly placed.

~Wisdom Series~

L

E

A

D

E

R

S

H

I

P

NUGGET 45

How do you know when God has placed you under the covering of a particular leadership or ministry? If they fall you stand in prayer.

We open ourselves up to error when we fail to see that our spiritual leaders are human beings first. Yes, there is a certain standard that an individual must uphold; more so when they are in leadership but they are not exempt from error. Does this mean that we condone it? No, God forbid: However, does it mean that we cover them in prayer. Yes!

NUGGET 46

Any leader that shows jealousy because of what you are becoming never became.

~Wisdom Series~

NUGGET 47

Be careful of the leader that is hesitant to embrace or acknowledge your future potential; because they want their now secured with your gifts and talents.

NUGGET 48

Any leader that won't release you to greater, thinks less of themselves.

NUGGET 49

True character is not based on intelligence, nor integrity alone.

Intelligence is foundation, integrity is graduation! Together they make a dynamic duo.

~Wisdom Series~

_L_

_A_

_Z_

_I_

_N_

_E_

_S_

_S_

~Wisdom Series~

NUGGET 50

Laziness is guaranteed to produce one sure thing, lack.
Proverbs 6:9

NUGGET 51

Your worth determines your wealth.

It is what you possess that determines your wealth. Who else can put a price on your hidden possessions but the one who owns them. Bill Gates is a man, what he possessed although hidden and overlooked at first made him a millionaire. A cave is only an empty pit until diamonds are found. Then it becomes a palace and a great fortress.

NUGGET 52

Hungry? Take notes from a bird. Even it knows where to find bread.
Give us this day our daily bread.
Matt 6:11

~Wisdom Series~

_L_

_O_

_V_

_E_

NUGGET 53

Adoration happens from time to time, but true love lasts forever.

NUGGET 54

Love is sometimes like a good umbrella. You never know how good it was until it made it through a rough wind.

NUGGET 55

The difference between lust and love is longevity! Lust wants commencement; loves requires commitment!

NUGGET 56

Never give all of yourself to the point where you can only find it in someone else!

Having a **big heart** and little or no discernment, can often lead to a **broken** one!

~Wisdom Series~

O

B

E

D

I

E

N

C

E

NUGGET 57

When God gives you specific directions, don't be persuaded by those who didn't hear him!

John 10:4, 5
For they (saints) know his voice and a stranger will not follow.

NUGGET 58

Wait can become weight and your failure to make haste could end up in waste. Pursue!

NUGGET 59

When you reject the gift of wisdom, You accept the penalties of ignorance.

Wisdom is like a posted Warning- Do Not Enter sign; take heed and live, neglect and wish you had.

NUGGET 60

A yes to God is produced when your no's are at their highest peak.

Opposition is many times your starting position for elevation.

NUGGET 61

What or who you sow into determines the value of the reward sown into you.

NUGGET 62

Like what you sow: you will have to deal with it again.

Be not deceived for God is not mocked; whatsoever a man soweth, that shall he also reap.

NUGGET 63

The presence of a storm in your situation can either be a contradiction or validation: you choose!

When Jesus commanded the disciples to get into the boat and go to the other side, little did they know that a storm would arise. Although the storm came their assignment did not change.

Rough winds, walls of waves and a brewing tide and undercurrent presented another opportunity to witness another side of God. They were obedient yet the storm came. Many times we think that the presence of a storm is an indication that you are in error.

Allow me to suggest to you that on the contrary storms can introduce your next promotion.!

~Wisdom Series~

_P_

_A_

_T_

_I_

_E_

_N_

_C_

_E_

NUGGET 64

Wait on God, or he'll have to wait on you.
Proverbs 3:5, 6

NUGGET 65

Anyone that yells didn't yield.

Have you ever been driving and trying to merge onto an interstate, highway or road and saw the yellow and black yield sign? Your failure to take a few moments to slow down and have <u>caution</u> could result in your being placed in a <u>coffin</u>.

Pray this:

Lord give me the grace, wisdom and direction to walk in temperance. Give me peace and clarity so that anxiety will not overtake me. Usher in calmness to my spirit so that I can be still and properly judge every situation and sound decisions.

~Wisdom Series~

P

L

A

N

S

NUGGET 66

Why just live when you can master your existence?

In the words of MLK be the best at whatever you do until you become the example.

NUGGET 67

Plans are God's witnesses when your faith is being tried!

Trials and tribulations don't change God's mind about what he spoke in the beginning. Plans are like your cheering squad, they encourage you to win.
Jeremiah 29:11

NUGGET 68

Complaint is the enemy of change.

~Wisdom Series~

POSSIBILITIES

NUGGET 69

Have you ever thought about this? A deaf individual can produce a hearing child.

Sometimes the impossible can produce the possible. Your own inability can produce another person's possibility. Be careful how you judge another individual because the real power and strength of that individual is not based on that which is seen.

If you didn't know Ray Charles or Stevie Wonder, you would feel a little sorry for them as they are escorted to the stage. However, in a few moments what was once your sympathy now becomes your celebration. Their display of talent and love for singing and playing would encourage and uplift. Remember this; weakness in one area could be a instrument of empowerment in another one!

~Wisdom Series~

P

R

A

I

S

E

NUGGET 70

Praise during pain is like a shelter during a tornado; you never know how bad it really was until it's over!

Psalm 34:19
Many are the afflictions of the righteous: but the LORD delivered him out of them all.

NUGGET 71

You don't praise God to get the victory but you praise him because by faith you've already seen the victory.

When you praise God on credit he'll take care of the balance!

~Wisdom Series~

NUGGET 72

Circumstances do not nor should they control your praise, but rather should intensify it!

Have you ever heard the cliché', 'God is good all the time and all the time God is good. Although like an adage used for many years, it expresses much truth. There is no situation that should be capable of robbing God of due praise. Any one can praise God when everything is going well, all the bills are paid, all relationships are in tack and there is money in the bank. However, it takes one that knows and understand that in everything God deserves praise Not necessarily for everything but while in it maintain a posture of praise.

You haven't praised God until you've praised him in a storm and it calms. You can either choose to be overcome by your circumstances, or overcome your circumstances with praise. One thing that is certain is whatever stands as an obstacle before praise shows up will always relent itself to becoming a mat under you. Praise is like a fixed fight, the victory is certain, just show up, with your hands up!

~Wisdom Series~

P
R
A
Y
E
R

~Wisdom Series~

NUGGET 73

If you want to catch up, get back on your knees. You'll get there much faster!

Prayer is like a time machine: Once you're in it prepare to be transformed to another place.

NUGGET 74

Prayer is like life-support; with it life is sure, without it death is almost certain.

NUGGET 75

Prayer in the life of a believer is what gasoline is to a car: It's dangerous when it gets low and when it runs out, you're left stranded.

~Wisdom Series~

NUGGET 76

Suffering from physical de-hydration? Try Gatorade. Suffering from spiritual de-hydration? Try <u>Prayer-Aide</u>.

What is Prayer?

P-**P**osition my self

R-to **R**eceive

A-**A**nswers

Y-that **Y**ield

E-sure **E**vidence

R-of my **R**elationship with God

~Wisdom Series~

_P_

_R_

_I_

_D_

_E_

NUGGET 77

Pride is putting a padlock on what has been preordained to be 'keyless-entry'.

Pride is a code that will never allow access into an open door but will cause you to remain behind closed doors!

Proverbs 16:18
Pride goes before destruction, and an haughty spirit before a fall.

Proverbs 29:23
A man's pride shall bring him low: but honor shall uphold the humble in spirit.

~Wisdom Series~

<u>P</u>

<u>R</u>

<u>O</u>

<u>C</u>

<u>E</u>

<u>S</u>

<u>S</u>

~Wisdom Series~

NUGGET 78

Have you ever thought about this? You enjoy olive oil, but were not there during the crushing.

Many people desire to be anointed but don't understand the true cost. They endeavor to be you until they find out what being you requires. They have no idea of the private battles, pain and sacrifices that one must endure. People want your glory but not your story!

NUGGET 79

Jesus is like a photographer. He deals with you in private; He sees all of your negatives but only allows the world to see the finished product.

Life with God is always a Kodak moment. Say 'cheese'!

~Wisdom Series~

NUGGET 80

When you're targeted for trouble, you're tagged for triumph.

Innocent of all wrong yet the Roman soldiers were <u>ordered</u> to whip Jesus to his knees, not knowing that one day they must fall to theirs'.

NUGGET 81

Even a pencil knows that it can't be sharpened without first shedding.

<u>Matthew 9:17</u>

Neither do men pour new wine into old wineskins. If they do, the skins will burst, the wine will run out and the wineskins will be ruined. No, they pour new wine into new wineskins, and both are preserved."

NUGGET 82

The future will never release you to a place that you cannot honor from where you are now.

NUGGET 83

Process is the bridge to success. Don't allow the altitude to deter you from crossing.

NUGGET 84

Anyone that often speaks of God's grace is an individual that has missed many graves.
Grace is God's extension towards us when we sin or fall short. Sin separates us from God and like playing rushing roulette without God's grace the chance for living is slim.

NUGGET 85

*No child starts walking at birth,
But God didn't wait to give it legs.*

2 Peter 1:3

³His divine power has given us everything we need for life and godliness through our knowledge of him who called us by his own glory and goodness.

NUGGET 86

It is difficult to become comfortable in a place you didn't intend on being. It is even more difficult to not learn the lesson and get further behind.

NUGGET 87

The past can do one or two things, <u>trap</u> you or <u>teach</u> you. You decide.

Your past should be a moment of reference while going forward and not a preference for staying where you are.

I have learned that when facing situations in life that it is better to learn what needs to be accomplished from an encounter and use it as foundation for future increase! A mistake is an opportunity to explore a more suitable way.

NUGGET 88

The only way your past can keep you is that you won't release it. The only way your future won't meet you is that you allow your past to defeat you. The difference between the past and the present is a moment. What you did five minutes ago is past unless you give it passage rights to invade your present or future.

~Wisdom Series~

PROCRASTINATION

NUGGET 89

Procrastination is like a disease; you either succumb to or take charge of it.

Procrastination is uncertainty, fate is surety. Procrastination is the speed you choose to obtain that which is already awaiting you. If you knew that there was a one million dollar check being held at your bank, would you walk, take a bicycle or drive your car?

Pray this:

Lord, help me to better understand the essence of time and to be an exceeding steward of it. Deliver me from my habitual carelessness and laziness so that I might see increase in my life. Help me to maximize every opportunity that presents itself and to be prepared for it. Cause me not to fear but to walk in confidence.

~Wisdom Series~

P

R

O

G

R

E

S

S

~Wisdom Series~

NUGGET 90

If you are behind schedule, get off of your behind.
Joshua 7:10

NUGGET 91

Rome was not built in one night, but it had to start one day.

The first step in doing anything is thought but the second one is action.

NUGGET 92

Even a baby recognizes when it needs a change!

Change may not always cause distress, but the unmet need for it can create an awful mess?

~Wisdom Series~

NUGGET 93

The price for going up is not giving up! Mistakes are the first steps to a guaranteed success.

Failing at things does not make you a failure. I was entered into my first talent show and bomb it because I was hoarse. I could have allowed that to stop me but now as I travel in and out of this country I'm glad I didn't give up.

NUGGET 94

Where there is no consistent movement there is no persistent life!

Movement determines progress but progress determines your overall success. Success is endured process!

Phil 3:14
I press towards the mark for the prize of the high calling of God in Christ Jesus.

~Wisdom Series~

P

R

O

V

I

S

I

O

N

NUGGET 95

When the Lord sent ravens to feed Elijah he didn't complain or give debate, he ate.

Philippians 4:19

But my God shall supply all your need according to his riches in glory by Christ Jesus.

NUGGET 96

God will sometimes use the unlikely to unleash the unexpected.

1 Kings 17:4

And it shall be that thou shalt drink of the brook; and I have commanded the ravens to feed thee there.

~Wisdom Series~

_P_

_U_

_R_

_P_

_O_

_S_

_E_

NUGGET 97

Purpose is to life what oxygen is to lungs. Though invisible is the driving force that gives vitality. One is fulfilled by the presence of the other.

What is purpose?

1. The reason for which something exists or is done, made, used, etc.
2. An intended or desired result; end; aim; goal.
3. Determination; resoluteness.

God did not create you as an afterthought or a plan b. You are you are a vital part of His plan in creation. Your uniqueness is a reflection of God's intent to impact the lives of those you come in contact with. You are God's idea! His plans are for you to prosper you and to bring you into an expected end. (Jer. 29:11).

~Wisdom Series~

REJECTION

NUGGET 98

Rejection is unsolicited direction that will save your life.

NUGGET 99

If you allow disrespect one time, expect it the next.

NUGGET 100

Only a fool walks directly into danger knowingly.

NUGGET 101

A lesson learned is an "A" earned!

Life is a school with many levels; only you can choose your date of graduation. The difference between what is earned and what is learned is the fact that one fills your mind; the other fills pockets. Either way, you'll have greater!

~Wisdom Series~

RELATIONSHIPS

~Wisdom Series~

NUGGET 102

When people walk out of the door of your life; voluntary or involuntarily, change the lock!

People must understand that once they are no longer apart of your life whether by your choice or theirs; they aren't allowed to just show up. It needs to be clear that what use to give them access no longer works! Your destiny depends on it.

NUGGET 103

Never burn a bridge; especially if you can't swim.

NUGGET 104

If you desire friends, start by being one.

Proverbs 18:24

A man that hath friends must show himself friendly: and there is a friend that sticketh closer than a brother.

NUGGET 105

If what has held you is still holding on, then what is assigned to you can't belong.

NUGGET 106

A bridge carries the cars, but the foundation upholds them both!
Oftentimes, the success of a thing is made possible by what is less seen. The bottom is not a bad place, because the top can't stand without it!

NUGGET 107

You attract what you are.
When is the last time you've seen a cat hanging out with a pack of dogs? Association brings impartation. Positive or negative, you choose!

~Wisdom Series~

THINKING

NUGGET 108

Frustration is a sign that your thoughts need changing so that your life can.

I used to get angry about my situation until one day I thought, how can I change this and what can I do differently? The problem certainly isn't going anywhere. Therefore the quicker you deal with it means the less you'll have to suffer because of it!

NUGGET 109

You can always turn E-V-I-L around and L-I-V-E a life of peace and harmony.

Romans 12:18

If it be possible, as much as lieth in you, live peaceably with all men.

~Wisdom Series~

T

I

M

I

N

G

NUGGET 110

Never make heaven's personal memos to you public information too soon!
Learn to close your mouth until the appropriate time. Everyone can't handle your success and favor.

NUGGET 111

It takes a mature individual that understands timing, to operate in the background: Especially when they know they belong on the front line.

NUGGET 112

The umbilical chord is a vital, but it too after serving its purpose must be cut off.
Ecclesiastes 3:1

NUGGET 113

Life will give you a song that everyone can sing.

NUGGET 114

Love is a choice that chance can't control.

No one enters into a meaningful relationship even if they believe that it is made in heaven thinking that there will not be challenges. However, once an individual allows themselves to be stripped of all barriers and apprehension, he or she commits to take every opportunity to make even greater ones.

The difference between making a choice and taking a chance is 'loyalty'. When making a choice, it will not change one's commitment even though the situation may change. In taking a chance, an individual's commitment and loyalty is only determined by the outcome.

~Wisdom Series~

BONUS

VITAMINS FOR YOUR VISION

FOR VISIONARIES & ENTREPENUERS

NUGGET 115

A man's vision is not activated by his thoughts; but by his pen.
Habakkuk 2:2

NUGGET 116

Where there is vision God gives provision. God will maintain what he ordained.
Since the creation in Genesis, have you ever witnessed anything that God spoke into existence stop existing?

NUGGET 117

True vision is standing in nothing but seeing everything.

NUGGET 125

The danger in making plans and then inviting God to the table for approval is that if he doesn't show up the deal goes bad.

NUGGET 126

You must be careful when and who you share your dreams with. What you let out at the wrong time may cost you your turn.

NUGGET 127

Where there is no personal investment, there is normally no total commitment.

NUGGET 128

The only difference between a millionaire and one who isn't is just a decision.

NUGGET 129

To whom much is given, much more is required. To who a little is given, more is also required.

NUGGET 130

Greatness is not determined by what you were born into, but rather what was placed inside of you.

Martin Luther King Jr. was born into racism, hate and injustice. However it did not stop him from making such an impact that even today causes celebration throughout this nation. The precise circumstance that challenged the essence of his ethnicity and identity was forced to CHANGE because of it!

NUGGET 131

The fear of the Lord is the beginning of knowledge, but fools despise wisdom and discipline.

NUGGET 132

Your dream's enemy is your destiny's validity.

It is rain that causes the umbrella's purpose to be fulfilled.

NUGGET 133

A man is not a man based on what he possesses, but rather what his vision is capable of producing.

NUGGET 134

One key formula for success is knowing that you you will very seldom have everyone's support.

NUGGET 135

Frustration and pressure is to prosperity what swollen ankles and morning sickness is to a pregnant woman; apart of the progress.

~Wisdom Series~

NUGGET 136

Why look up to someone who desires to hold you down? Your misplaced loyalties can hinder future royalties.

NUGGET 137

Never sell out to someone who walked out. This best partner to have in one that stays positioned beside you, in spite of opposing conditions surrounding you!

NUGGET 138

Unlike a brand new car, people who walk away from you have just added to your value. People that walk away from what looks like black dirt, disqualifies themselves: as partakers when they discover that after being polished, the coal was a fortune of diamonds.

NUGGET 139

If you're the smartest person in your circle, the circle is too small. The best way to be smarter is to surround yourself with people that make you feel dumb!

You have not reached a level of success until those that surround you are encouraged, empowered and dumfounded by you, until then make sure that you are surrounded by people who make you feel stupid. Iron sharpens iron

NUGGET 140

Knowledge is realizing the importance of marching to the beat of a different drummer. Wisdom is learning how to beat your own.

What a wonderful thing to be different; what an even better thing to make a difference.

~Wisdom Series~

NUGGET 141

Be careful of the people that praise you. They'll often time be the same ones to raise you!

Remember when Jesus rode in on a donkey thee people praised him saying 'hosanna'; but by the end of the story the same people said crucify him and sentenced him to be raised on the cross!

Mark 11:9

And they that went before, and they that followed, cried, saying, Hosanna; Blessed is he that cometh in the name of the Lord:

NUGGET 142

Never allow a person to use your vulnerability as an opportunity to claim accountability.

People will use your innocence and make it there indulgence. In the end they'll try to take all the credit and leave you with deficit.

NUGGET 143

Trusting people is like accepting a counterfeit check; you let them in and they bounce.
Real trust, can be traced.

NUGGET 144

Be careful of who you allow to invest in your life because what was a personal and private investment to you can be a large bank withdrawal for them later on.

NUGGET 145

Real trust, can be traced
Never allow someone's ill intention to prevent your dream.

NUGGET 146

Even a dog won't eat certain foods. Not even hunger will change his mind.
James 1:8

NUGGET 147

Look at this carefully, the poor you shall have with you always.
With you is not you!
Poverty is a mind set that will sit you in a different place: Once there, allow compassion to cause you to be a blessing to others.

NUGGET 148

If God really needed your help, where were you in Genesis?
God doesn't need your help to show his God-ness, but requires your faith so that he can prove his goodness.

NUGGET 149

It takes a mature individual that understands God's timing to operate in the background when they've been given a 'front line' anointing.

NUGGET 149-Continued

David had been given a kingly anointing but still had to maintain a peasant position. This would have been an embarrassment to the individual whose motive was to have popularity and fame; It was not until David had completed his assignment on earth, that he was granted the privilege of stepping into heaven's intended purpose for him. The completion of his earthly commission was his process that prepared him for admission to his next level.

Process is the test that will get out of you God's best!

If you will give God time he will make sure that you get your turn. Everything has its time and launching. The right move executed at the wrong time can and will be detrimental.

NUGGET 150

Before you hurdle stones at one that has fallen, remember that there are more stones.

NUGGET 150

My brothers and I use to have snow ball and dirt bomb fights. It was an exciting escapade to hit them, but the moment one hit me on the side the head, the game wasn't so exciting. Just when you want to judge and sentence one that has made a mistake; remember that but by the grace of God you could be in the similar situation. Laughing is fun until you're the one being laughed that and then it's not so funny.

NUGGET 151

One day's mistake can cause a lifetime of misery. You'll spend years knowing it wasn't worth it.

NUGGET 152

If at the end of the day you are 'dog' tired, could it be because you've been <u>barking</u> all day?
Prov. 15:1

A soft answer turneth away wrath: but grievous words stir up anger.

NUGGET 153

Anything unappreciated will leave. Whatever you appreciate will increase.

NUGGET 154

Vision at first is often lonely, until it produces results.

Isn't it amazing how when building a vision no one can be found but when it is manifested the whole world comes around?

NUGGET 155

Complacency is devastation's most active ingredient.

NUGGET 156

Tough decisions are often the result of making bad ones.

NUGGET 157

The greatest mistake is being busy but not being productive. There is a difference.

Success is not how well you spend your money but rather your time.

NUGGET 158

Watch your surroundings carefully; an instigator is often a perpetuator with a mask.

NUGGET 159

Success is not predicated by what society determines but by what your vision demands.
Never allow people to place you into a certain stereotype when you can create your own class.

NUGGET 160

What you are in life right now is the harvest of the time you have invested into yourself before now.

On my 31st birthday I awakened depressed although I should have been jubilant. I thought about my age and all that God had allowed me to accomplish and realized one important thing; It was all for someone else. I had helped people build churches, record albums, start business, etc and I had nothing tangible to show for it. I realized right then that it was time now to invest into my dreams, hope and aspirations. What made it more difficult was the fact that I was forgotten and perhaps not even a memory to those that I had supported. I realized that if I could help them, I could do it my self.

> Take the time to build yourself. At this point it is not about being selfish. What you have deposited into the lives of others is evidence that you are not nor have been selfish or egotistical. There comes a time where you must no longer allow yourself to be charity but a rarity. Your success and destiny depends on it!

~Wisdom Series~

NUGGET 161

If you fail to clean up the mess of your yesterday, you may very well end up stepping in it tomorrow! Anything no good to know becomes <u>waste</u> and if not corrected in time will cause you to <u>waste</u> valuable time.

NUGGET 162

Your 'coming attraction' could be a green light for your destiny's assassin!

Although your vision is huge and you know how the Kingdom will be enhanced because of it; it is sometimes best to SHUT YOUR MOUTH until the time of unveiling. This does not mean you are afraid of your enemy but SMARTER!

NUGGET 163

A person seldom regrets leaving a 'never mind', until the 'never mind' become a goldmine; typically someone else's

NUGGET 164

Excuses are like weeds...they grow up with you and then try to kill you!

NUGGET 165

A man's gift will never make room for him if he refuses to come out of the box! A seed left in the bag is useless until deposited into the earth.

NUGGET 166

Never leave your assignment without being properly released. There is nothing right about wrong.

NUGGET 167

A mediocre attitude, will always be the adversary that keeps you from ever reaching extraordinary altitudes.

NUGGET 168

You never have to make destiny happen. You must make the right decisions that will prepare you for it!

An open door is better when prepared for than hoped for.

NUGGET 169

Which one is better, the nail or the hammer? Neither, they rely on each other to fulfill their purpose. A prideful person is often a lonely one.

The only person that thinks he or she does not need anyone is a person that has isolated themselves from everyone.

NUGGET 170

Limitation is a condition that only liber-heal. Get freedom! It will pay for

~Wisdom Series~

NUGGET 171

Success in the wrong thing is failure with 'bling bling'.

NUGGET 172

What you entertain becomes your name. You're identified by what comes from inside.

NUGGET 173

The only difference between a stop light and stop sign is that both are to be respected but one at will the other at command.

What you don't demand you will never get. Some things should be an option but some things don't have a choice.

~Wisdom Series~

And more…

~Wisdom Series~

BECOME

A

GLOBAL PARTNER

TODAY & HELP US

CHANGE THE WORLD

ONE WORD AT A TIME!